DATE DUE

EXTREME
MOTO X

Heather C. Hudak

W

Weigl Publishers Inc.

Published by Weigl Publishers Inc.
350 5th Avenue, Suite 3304, PMB 6G
New York, NY 10118-0069

Website: www.weigl.com

Library of Congress Cataloging-in-Publication Data available upon request.
Fax 1-866-44-WEIGL for the attention of the Publishing Records department.

ISBN 978-1-59036-914-2 (hard cover)
ISBN 978-1-59036-915-9 (soft cover)

Printed in the United States of America
1 2 3 4 5 6 7 8 9 0   12 11 10 09 08

Weigl would like to acknowledge Getty Images as its primary photo supplier for this title.

EDITOR: Heather C. Hudak
DESIGN: Terry Paulhus
LAYOUT: Kathryn Livingstone

EXTREME MOTO X

CONTENTS

WHAT ARE THE X GAMES?

The X Games are an annual sports tournament that showcases the best athletes in the extreme sports world. Extreme sports are performed at high speeds. Participants must wear special equipment to help protect them from injury. Only athletes who spend years training should take part in these sports. There are many competitions, such as the X Games, that celebrate the skill, dedication, and determination of the athletes, as well as the challenge and difficulty of the sports.

TECHNOLINK

Learn more about the X Games at **expn.go.com**.

The X Games began as the Extreme Games in 1995. The following year, the name was shortened to X Games. In 1995 and 1996, the games were held in the summer, and they featured a wide variety of sports. These included skateboarding, inline skating, BMX, street luge, sky surfing, and rock climbing.

The popularity of the X Games made it possible for more sports to be showcased. In 1997, the Winter X Games began. The Winter X Games feature sports such as snowboarding, skiing, and snowmobiling. Today, there are Summer and Winter X Games each year.

Some of the best motocross, or moto X, riders in the world compete in the X Games. These athletes perform extreme moves in front of large crowds. Events feature riders flying through the air or racing at high speeds.

X FEST

The X Games are about more than sports. Each year, musical acts from all over the world perform for fans at the X Games. X Fest is the name for the musical portion of the X Games. It features some of the best-known punk rock, hip hop, and alternative music artists of the time. These artists perform between sporting events and keep the crowds entertained and excited

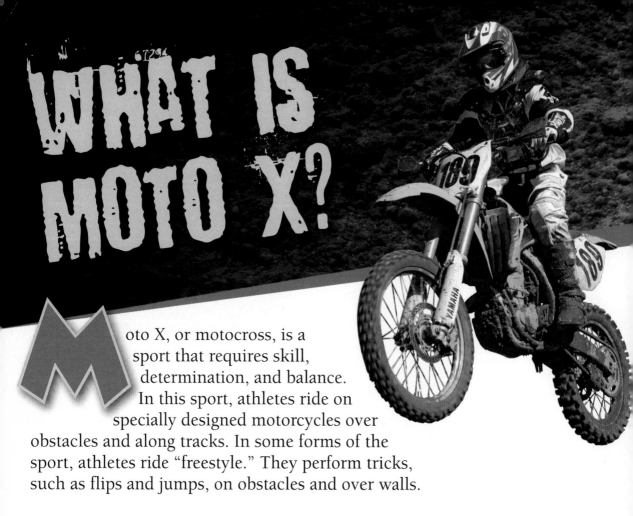

WHAT IS MOTO X?

Moto X, or motocross, is a sport that requires skill, determination, and balance. In this sport, athletes ride on specially designed motorcycles over obstacles and along tracks. In some forms of the sport, athletes ride "freestyle." They perform tricks, such as flips and jumps, on obstacles and over walls.

At the X Games, there are several freestyle events, including Best Trick, Step Up, and Freestyle. There also are races, such as **SuperMoto** and Moto X Racing, in which groups of riders start at the same time along dirt and pavement courses. They must face **whoops** and large jumps as they race to the finish.

Timeline

1885 – Gottlieb Daimler designs a motor bicycle that has wooden wheels and a combustion engine.

1924 – The first Scrambles takes place at Camberley, Surrey.

1959 – The first moto X races are held in the United States.

1969 – The sport gets wide exposure when it is featured on ABC's *Wide World of Sports*.

1972 – The first stadium motocross event is held at the Los Angeles Coliseum.

1975 – The 125cc world championship contributes to the growth of moto X and leads to an increase in popularity of sport in the United States.

Moto X is based on a British **off-road** sport known as the Scrambles. Athletes rode motorcycles over dirt trails. The first-known Scrambles event was held in 1924 at Camberley, Surrey, in Great Britain.

Over time, the event changed. European competitions included shorter tracks, more laps, and various obstacles throughout the course. The bikes held up poorly in the tough conditions, and specially designed bikes became part of the sport. As the events and the tracks became more difficult, motorcycles became more advanced and lightweight. These bikes were made to withstand a great deal of wear and tear.

Moto X races are held throughout the United States.

Soon, moto X gained popularity in the United States. New forms of riding were added to traditional competitions. These included indoor arena events, such as **Supercross** and Freestyle moto X, where riders show off many riding skills.

990 – Moto X begins to nclude indoor stadium events, nown as Supercross and renacross. Freestyle (FMX) vents, where riders are judged n their jumping and aerial crobatic skills, gain popularity.

1998 – Moto X starts as a demonstration sport at the X Games.

1999 – Moto X freestyle becomes an X Games sport. Riders are allowed 90 seconds to complete a course of ramps of different heights, lengths, and angles.

2000 – Tommy Clowers wins the first-ever X Games moto X Step Up event.

2006 – Travis Pastrana lands the first-ever double back flip in the X Games Best Trick final event.

ALL THE RIGHT EQUIPMENT

Moto X riding is often done on public land. In these places, there are dirt trails and jumps where riders can practice tricks. Natural elements, such as mud holes, rocky ledges, and steep hills are used as obstacles.

Whether they are taking part in a competition or riding for pleasure, riders wear moto X suits that offer protection against falls. Suits include long-sleeve jerseys that fit over top of protective gear and long, padded pants. Moto X is a dangerous sport, so it is important for riders to take additional precautions.

To prevent harming their rib cage and internal organs, riders wear chest protectors. These hard plastic vests act as a shield across the rider's breastbone. A full-face shield is worn to protect the rider's face and eyes from the rocks and mud that are kicked up by the moving bike. Knee and elbow guards are hard plastic covers that strap to the joints and help prevent major injuries.

ACCESSORIZE IT !

Many riders wear goggles and gloves. These protect their eyes and hands from dirt that flies up from the track. To land safely, riders need to see clearly as they make jumps and stunts. Goggles ensure they can do this. Gloves help the riders grip the bike's handles, seats, and other parts of the motorcycle when riders fly through the air. Gloves also protect the rider's hands if they fall in the hard dirt.

The helmet is the most important piece of safety equipment. When falling off a motorbike, a rider's head can hit the ground. Helmets have saved riders from serious head injury.

The long, flat seat on the bike is designed to allow riders to shift their weight quickly and provide more **traction** in corners.

Moto X machines have plenty of **suspension** to allow riders to tackle large jumps and ride at a higher speed over the rough course. To bring the weight of the bike down, parts, such as speedometers, lights, and kickstands, are removed from most machines.

Most bikes for moto X are smaller than traditional motorcycles. A moto X bike can be a two-stroke or a four-stroke machine. Two-stroke bikes are lighter, more powerful, and noisier than four-stroke bikes, but the are less environmentally friendly.

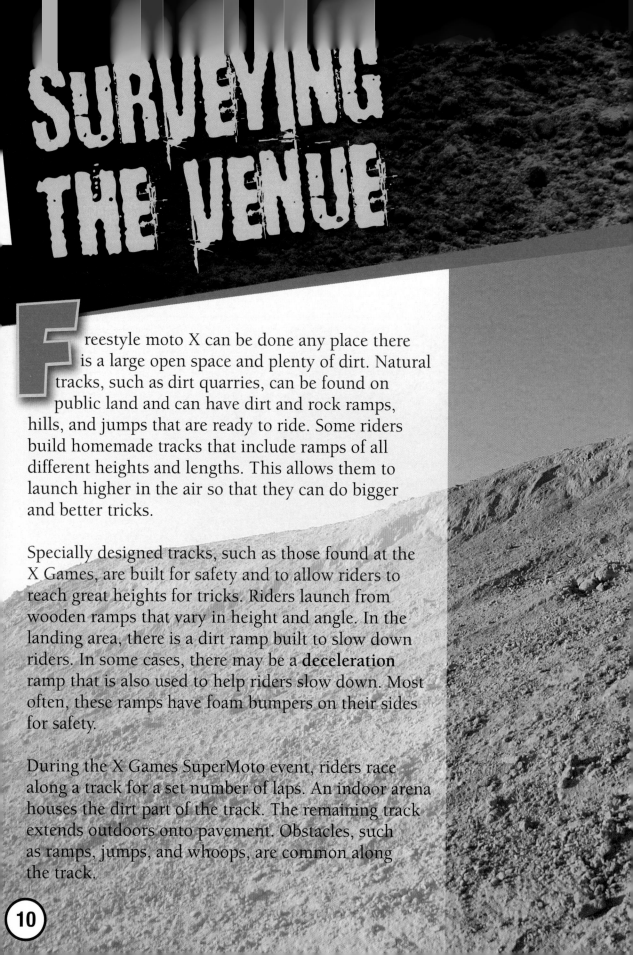

SURVEYING THE VENUE

Freestyle moto X can be done any place there is a large open space and plenty of dirt. Natural tracks, such as dirt quarries, can be found on public land and can have dirt and rock ramps, hills, and jumps that are ready to ride. Some riders build homemade tracks that include ramps of all different heights and lengths. This allows them to launch higher in the air so that they can do bigger and better tricks.

Specially designed tracks, such as those found at the X Games, are built for safety and to allow riders to reach great heights for tricks. Riders launch from wooden ramps that vary in height and angle. In the landing area, there is a dirt ramp built to slow down riders. In some cases, there may be a **deceleration** ramp that is also used to help riders slow down. Most often, these ramps have foam bumpers on their sides for safety.

During the X Games SuperMoto event, riders race along a track for a set number of laps. An indoor arena houses the dirt part of the track. The remaining track extends outdoors onto pavement. Obstacles, such as ramps, jumps, and whoops, are common along the track.

Desert terrain makes for good riding conditions.

TECHNOLINK

To find out more about moto X, visit **www.motocross.com**.

BEST TRICK

The most extreme moto X competition in the X Games is called Best Trick. Ten riders each take two jumps off a dirt-covered ramp. After launching off the ramp, the riders perform tricks in the air and land on another dirt ramp that helps them slow down. Riders execute a variety of tricks in the Best Trick competition, including backflips, corkscrews, and front flips.

In this event, the rider who performs the most impressive trick wins the event. A panel of 10 judges scores the riders' style, trick difficulty, and use of the course. Riders are scored individually on a scale of 1 to 10 for each of their jumps, and only their highest score is counted toward the final prize. The top-scoring rider wins the Best Trick event.

Dayne Kinnaird has competed in many X Games.

BEST TRICK PAST WINNERS

2007
Gold — Kyle Loza
Silver — Adam Jones
Bronze — Todd Potter

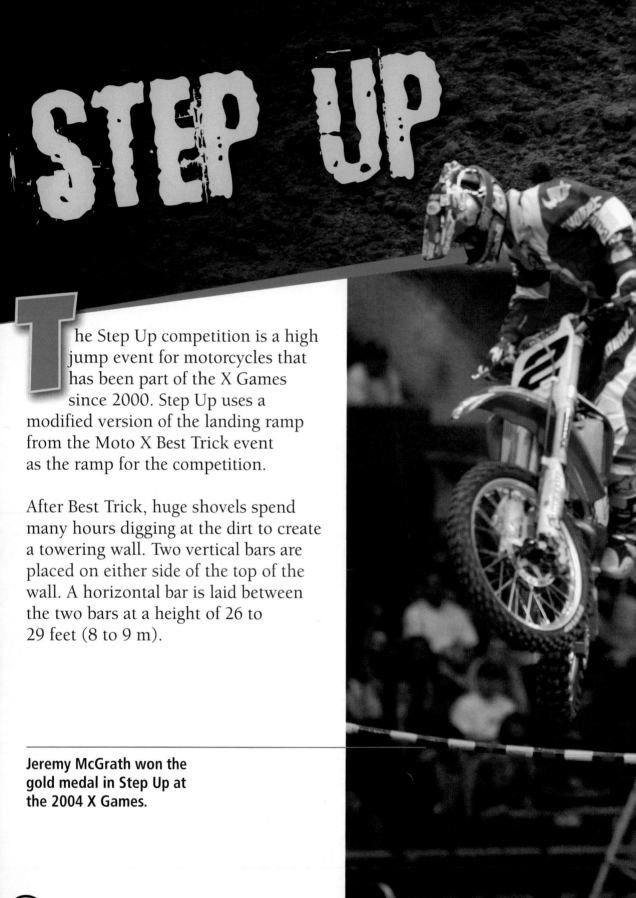

STEP UP

The Step Up competition is a high jump event for motorcycles that has been part of the X Games since 2000. Step Up uses a modified version of the landing ramp from the Moto X Best Trick event as the ramp for the competition.

After Best Trick, huge shovels spend many hours digging at the dirt to create a towering wall. Two vertical bars are placed on either side of the top of the wall. A horizontal bar is laid between the two bars at a height of 26 to 29 feet (8 to 9 m).

Jeremy McGrath won the gold medal in Step Up at the 2004 X Games.

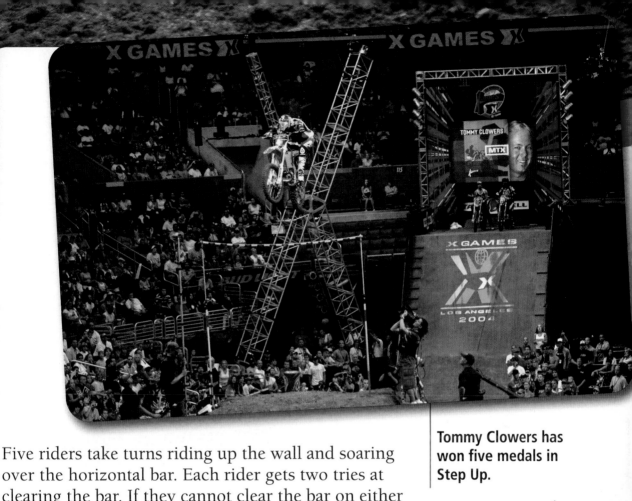

Five riders take turns riding up the wall and soaring over the horizontal bar. Each rider gets two tries at clearing the bar. If they cannot clear the bar on either try, they are eliminated from the event. Once each rider has attempted the jump, the bar is raised 6 inches (15 centimeters), and the competition starts again. This continues until only one rider remains.

Tommy Clowers has won five medals in Step Up.

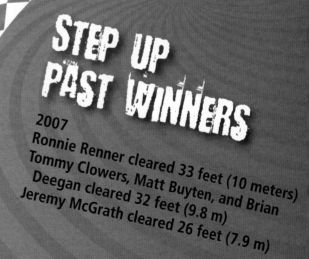

STEP UP PAST WINNERS

2007
Ronnie Renner cleared 33 feet (10 meters)
Tommy Clowers, Matt Buyten, and Brian Deegan cleared 32 feet (9.8 m)
Jeremy McGrath cleared 26 feet (7.9 m)

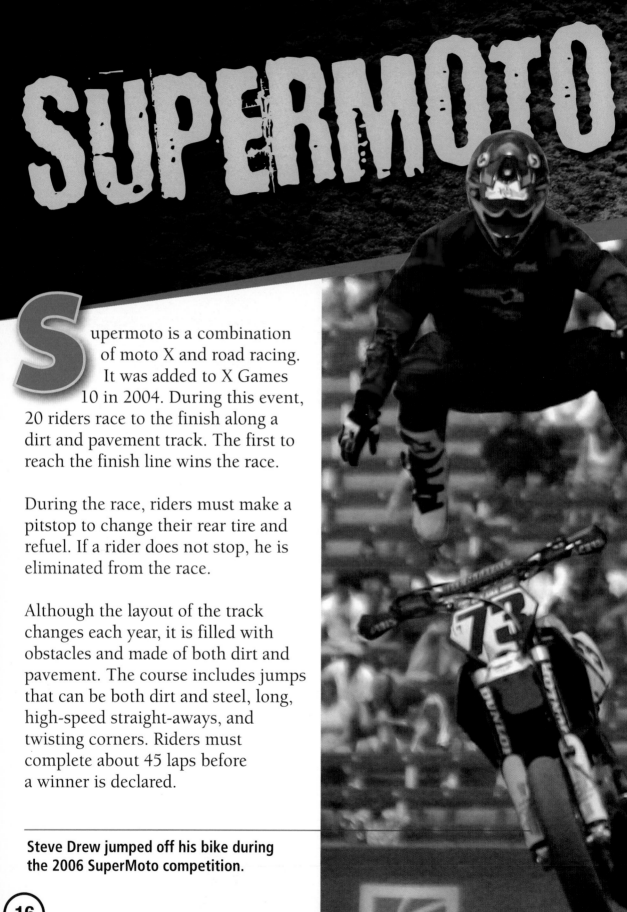

SUPERMOTO

Supermoto is a combination of moto X and road racing. It was added to X Games 10 in 2004. During this event, 20 riders race to the finish along a dirt and pavement track. The first to reach the finish line wins the race.

During the race, riders must make a pitstop to change their rear tire and refuel. If a rider does not stop, he is eliminated from the race.

Although the layout of the track changes each year, it is filled with obstacles and made of both dirt and pavement. The course includes jumps that can be both dirt and steel, long, high-speed straight-aways, and twisting corners. Riders must complete about 45 laps before a winner is declared.

Steve Drew jumped off his bike during the 2006 SuperMoto competition.

Jeremy McGrath led the pack at the beginning of the SuperMoto race in 2004. He took third place.

SUPERMOTO PAST WINNERS

2007
Gold – Mark Burkhart
Silver – Jeff Ward
Bronze – David Pingree

QUALIFYING TO COMPETE

The first step to becoming a professional moto X rider is to get sponsored. Companies sponsor riders by paying them to wear their brand name or logo at competitions or in TV and magazine advertisements selling the company's product. X Games athletes do not need a sponsor to take part in the games, but they do need money for equipment, travel, and living expenses while they train for events. To become sponsored, a person must be very good at moto X. Riders who perform never-before-seen tricks and push themselves to try new stunts are more likely to get noticed by sponsoring companies.

TECHNOLINK

To learn how to ride moto X, check out **www.dirtrider.com/index.html**.

Sometimes, companies will approach athletes about sponsorship. However, most companies will not know about a good rider unless that person is competing at big events. For this reason, many riders contact companies about sponsorship.

Once a rider has been noticed and has competed in other events, he or she may be ready to compete in the X Games. Only the gold medalist from the previous X Games receives a guaranteed invitation to compete. To select the other competitors, a committee is formed. It decides which athletes to invite to compete at the X Games. The decision is based on three **criteria**.

First, the committee reviews the results from all major freestyle moto X events. Riders with top scores are more likely to be invited to the X Games. Next, the committee looks at which athletes have received a great deal of attention from the **media**. These athletes are crowd favorites, and many people will watch the event just to see these people perform. Finally, riders who show great skill and have spent a great deal of time in the sport will get a chance to compete.

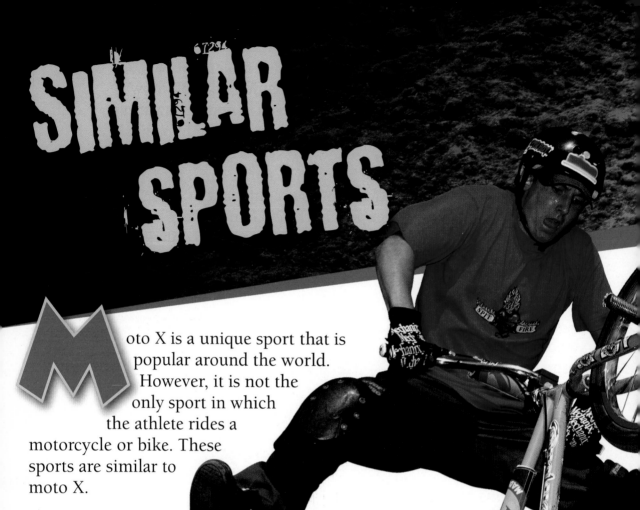

SIMILAR SPORTS

Moto X is a unique sport that is popular around the world. However, it is not the only sport in which the athlete rides a motorcycle or bike. These sports are similar to moto X.

BMX

In BMX, or bicycle moto X, athletes use specially designed bicycles to race or to perform stunts. BMX can be done on almost any type of surface, including dirt or concrete. Like skateboarders and snowboarders, many freestyle BMX riders use rails, ramps, jumps, and other obstacles to perform tricks. BMX racers speed along dirt tracks. The first rider to reach the finish line wins the race. BMX first started in California in the 1970s, when children and teens would try to copy moto X tricks on regular bikes.

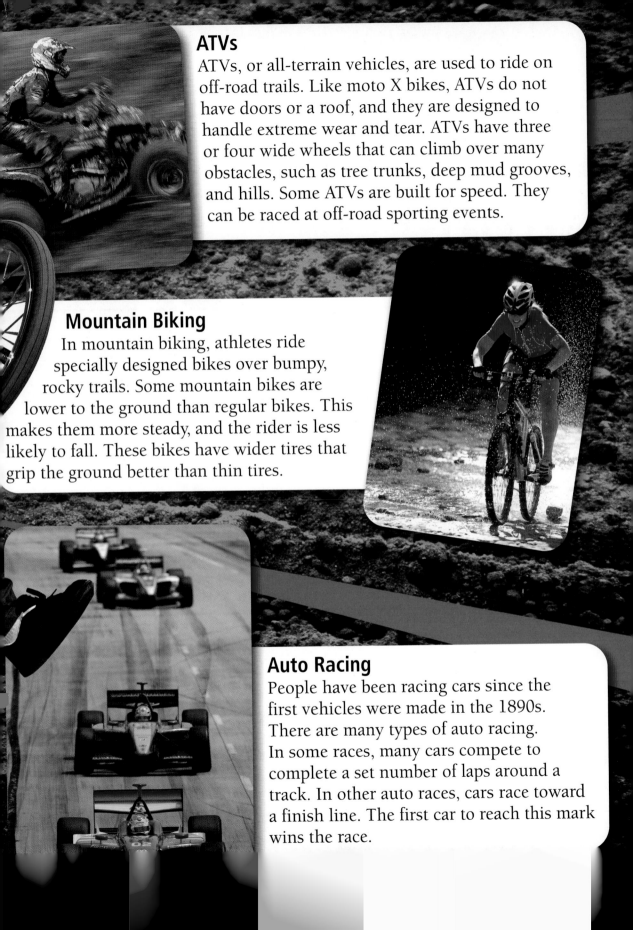

ATVs

ATVs, or all-terrain vehicles, are used to ride on off-road trails. Like moto X bikes, ATVs do not have doors or a roof, and they are designed to handle extreme wear and tear. ATVs have three or four wide wheels that can climb over many obstacles, such as tree trunks, deep mud grooves, and hills. Some ATVs are built for speed. They can be raced at off-road sporting events.

Mountain Biking

In mountain biking, athletes ride specially designed bikes over bumpy, rocky trails. Some mountain bikes are lower to the ground than regular bikes. This makes them more steady, and the rider is less likely to fall. These bikes have wider tires that grip the ground better than thin tires.

Auto Racing

People have been racing cars since the first vehicles were made in the 1890s. There are many types of auto racing. In some races, many cars compete to complete a set number of laps around a track. In other auto races, cars race toward a finish line. The first car to reach this mark wins the race.

UNFORGETTABLE MOMENTS

Throughout the history of the X Games, there have been many unforgettable moments. These include record-breaking wins, long falls, and new tricks.

At the Winter X Games in 2004, Brian Deegan crashed hard during the Best Trick competition. Deegan was favored to win the event, after winning the gold medal at the previous Summer X Games and medalling at Winter X Games 6 as well. During the **preliminary** round, Deegan planned to land one of his newest moves, a 360-degree rotation in the air. Soon after takeoff, he knew he could not execute the trick. Instead, he jumped from his bike and fell 45 feet (14 m) onto the hard snow. Deegan broke both wrists and his femur. To the surprise of many moto X fans and athletes, Deegan quickly recovered from his injuries. The following year, he returned to the X Games and took home the gold medal for Best Trick.

Mike Metzger made history at the 2002 X Games. By now, performing flips on bikes was a common feat for top riders. To get noticed, riders had to try bigger and better stunts. In the last few seconds of his 90-second Best Trick run, Metzger decided to boost his routine. He raced toward a 10-foot (3-m) ramp at high speed and performed a backflip. After touching down, Metzger sped toward another ramp and landed a second flip. This was the first time a rider had landed two backflips in a row. Metzger took home the gold in both the Best Trick and Freestyle events, as well as a silver in Step Up.

At the 2006 X Games, Travis Pastrana became the first person to land a double backflip in competition. The double backflip is currently considered the most difficult freestyle trick. After landing the trick, Pastrana vowed never to try it again. He competed in four events at the games and took home the gold medal in three.

Victoria, Canada

Natural paths and rugged terrain near Victoria provide excellent obstacles, such as dirt jumps, natural ramps, and long gorges.

ATLANTIC OCEAN

Baja, Mexico

The deserts, dunes, and beaches of Mexico allow for an exciting riding experience. A trip through Baja to Mike's Sky Ranch or Cabo San Lucas requires more riding experience.

PACIFIC OCEAN

Ocotillo Wells, California

Ocotillo Wells State Vehicle Recreation Area is a California State Park that caters to off-road vehicle riders. The park features more than 80,000 acres (32,375 hectares) of land for riding, as well as free camping.

Games Venues

1. Rhode Island, United States
2. Los Angeles, United States
3. Mexico City, Mexico
4. Rio de Janeiro, Brazil
5. Kuala Lumpur, Malaysia
6. Shanghai, China

ARCTIC
OCEAN

ARCTIC
OCEAN

Prague, Czech Republic

Aside from a professional area for moto X in Prague, there are many trails and natural paths through the surrounding woods. The terrain is hilly and good for jumping.

Dubai, Persian Gulf

In Dubai, people can go "dune bashing," taking off-road vehicles and dirt bikes out into the desert.

PACIFIC
OCEAN

INDIAN
OCEAN

South East Queensland's Black Duck Valley, Australia

South East Queensland's Black Duck Valley, located 90 minutes from Brisbane, offers natural trails that overlook mountain ranges and rocky terrain, as well as a park with tracks and freestyle ramps.

CURRENT STARS

NATE ADAMS

HOMETOWN
Phoenix, Arizona

BORN
March 29, 1984

NOTES
Won his first freestyle championship at age 18

The first rider to execute a back flip with a no-hander landing in competition, and the first moto X rider to beat Travis Pastrana at a freestyle moto X event

Is the title character in a cell phone video game

TRAVIS PASTRANA

HOMETOWN
Annapolis, Maryland

BORN
October 8, 1983

NOTES
Won gold medals in Supercross, moto X, and freestyle moto X

Always races on Suzuki motorcycles that carry the number 199

Featured in the moto X stunt video *Travis and the Nitro Circus*

BRIAN DEEGAN

HOMETOWN
Omaha, Nebraska,

BORN
May 9, 1975

NOTES
Has won 10 gold
medals—the most in
FMX X Games history

Has a toy line called Heavy Hitters

Is featured in a card and dice game
called Battle FMX

MIKE METZGER

HOMETOWN
Huntington Beach,
California

BORN
November 19, 1975

NOTES
Won the 2002 Freestyle
and Best Trick events and
took second place in Step Up

Completed a world record backflip
over the fountains in front of
Caesar's Palace hotel in Las Vegas

Appears in an moto X racing video
game called *Freakstyle*

LEGENDS

RICKY CARMICHAEL

HOMETOWN
Havana, Florida

BORN
November 27, 1979

NOTES
Known as the G.O.A.T., or the Greatest of all Time

First competed in the X Games in 2007 and won gold

Holds the most records of any moto X rider

CAREY HART

HOMETOWN
Seal Beach, California

BORN
July 17, 1975

NOTES
Became a professional moto X rider at the age of 17

Began riding freestyle full-time when he was 23

Signature trick is the "Hart Attack," a backflip

Owns the Hart and Huntington tattoo chain

CHUCK CAROTHERS

HOMETOWN
Hattiesburg, Massachusetts

BORN
June 20, 1978

NOTES
Won gold at X Games 4 when he landed a body varial, or "**Carolla**"

Has had 21 broken bones and 13 surgeries

Lives at "Camp Chuck," where he has a foam pit for moto X practice

JEREMY STENBERG

HOMETOWN
San Diego, California

BORN
September 27, 1981

NOTES
Won gold at X Games 10 for Best Trick

Has won two X Games gold medals, two Gravity Games silver medals, two X Fighters silver medals, an Air and Style silver medal, and an LG Action Sports silver medal

Started riding at the age of two when his dad gave him a motorcycle for Christmas

THE 10 QUESTION QUIZ

1. In what year were the first X games held?

2. Where were the first moto X races held?

3. When was the first moto X ever held at the X Games?

4. What is the most important piece of safety equipment for a rider?

5. What are SuperMoto tracks made from?

6. Who landed the first-ever double backflip at the X Games?

7. How many riders compete in Best Trick?

8. How many inches is the bar raised each round of a Step Up competiti[on]?

9. Who performed the first ever back[flip] on full-size moto X bike?

10. Who is guaranteed an invitation to compete in the X Games?

Answers: 1. 1995 2. Camberley, Surrey, [i]n Great Britain 3. 1999 4. helmet 5. dirt and pavement 6. Travis Pastrana 7. 10 [8]. 6 inches (15 cm) 9. Carey Hart 10. the [g]old medalist from the previous X Games